Football Grounds Fr...
Floodl...

by Mike Flo...

Published by Newlands Photographic,
71 Stones Cross Road, Crockenhill, Swanley, Kent BR8 8LT

Text, concept, images and layout © Mike Floate 2016

All rights reserved. No part of this publication may be reproduced or copied in any manner without the permission of the publisher.

<u>Above</u>: Sunset over the Pilot Field, Hastings United FC, January 1991.

ISBN 978-1-900257-28-2

Printed and bound by Catford Print Centre

Introduction

They took all the trees
And put them in a tree museum
And they charged all the people
A dollar and a half to see 'em

Back in 1970 Joni Mitchell's environmentally-aware song Big Yellow Taxi spoke of a tree museum in the USA. Back then I'd have scoffed at the suggestion that we'd have something similar in the UK. What did I know? Yet the Eden Project is exactly the sort of place that the song describes.

Listening to the song I would also have said that one structure which I and everyone else took for granted would never be included in a museum: a floodlight from a Football League ground. I'd have said: 'and there won't be a song about one, nor a book – surely not?'. What did I know? There may never be a song or museum but here is the book.

I just accepted floodlights as being part of a football ground from the first game I went to on a Wednesday evening in 1964 at Selhurst Park.

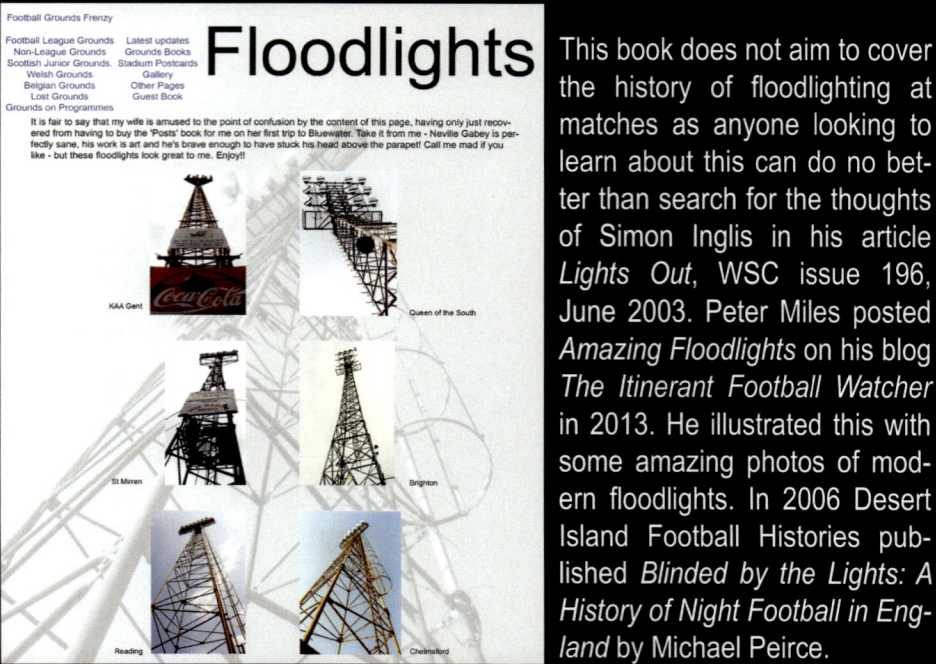

This book does not aim to cover the history of floodlighting at matches as anyone looking to learn about this can do no better than search for the thoughts of Simon Inglis in his article *Lights Out*, WSC issue 196, June 2003. Peter Miles posted *Amazing Floodlights* on his blog *The Itinerant Football Watcher* in 2013. He illustrated this with some amazing photos of modern floodlights. In 2006 Desert Island Football Histories published *Blinded by the Lights: A History of Night Football in England* by Michael Peirce.

My intention is to use images to record the amazing variety of floodlights which I have come across at football grounds, which at first glance may all appear to be very similar. On closer inspection one can note that engineers have used different sections of steel, different ways of triangulating to add strength, different means of holding back corrosion, different footprints from which to build their pylons, to different heights, with different means of supplying the power and with different ways of mounting different numbers of differing lamps. They even offer different means of accessing the lamps, ensuring that service engineers are protected and that unauthorised people do not climb the pylons.

Some clubs mount adverts on their pylons while some use them to mount devices such as loudspeakers or to route cables between stands. They are mostly in the same general position but never exactly the same distance from the corner of the ground. Only one club felt the need to add floodlights on the halfway line, while others began the current trend for mounting their lights on the roof of a stand. I will draw no further attention to these points but leave the reader to investigate for themselves. I may even have failed to note some differences myself.

Left: My original Grounds Frenzy website was the first to feature floodlights in 1999.

Right: Hastings United were so pleased to host evening games that a generic floodlight adorned their programme.

Below: Subbuteo for me was non-League as I didn't aim to buy the floodlighting set.

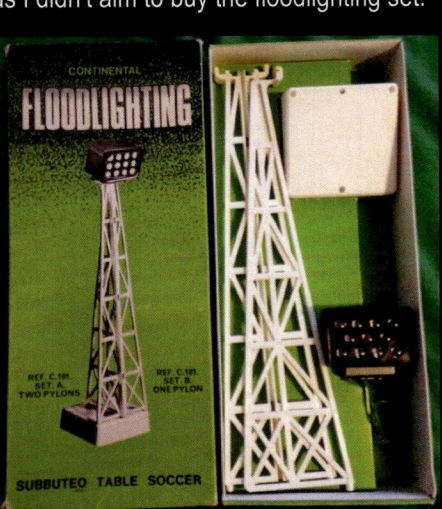

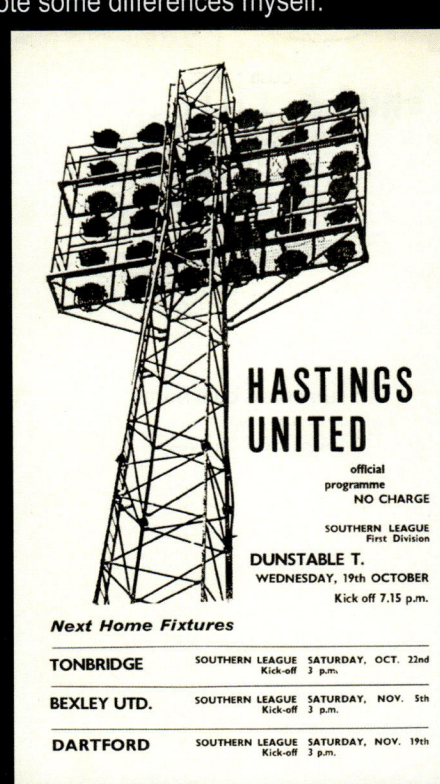

When travelling it was always possible to spot town-centre grounds from a train or car. I can still look out for the floodlights at the Crystal Palace National Sports Centre every time I travel by train to London. On arrival at a station the direction in which to walk was often clear to see, or an idea gained by seeing the floodlights on the way in. Visiting spectators in cars could judge when to park and walk the remaining distance to an away ground.

There is always an exception. When planning a visit to Gillingham I asked my Millwall-supporting friend the best way to get to the game. His reply was priceless. 'I dunno, when we go anywhere we just stop, wind down the window and demand 'Oi, we're Millwall: where's the ground?'.

My archive of images began when I visited Queen of the South in 1996, with the most recent image being added in 2015. Although most of the floodlights featured illuminated Football League matches I have also included Scottish, non-League and Belgian floodlights. Other than Bristol Rovers, whose floodlight was seen to be lighting the delivery bay of the IKEA store built on the site of Eastville, I have made no specific journeys to gather these images.

Boston United

Today there are fewer traditional floodlight pylons with many clubs opting to replace them with modern and less photogenic tubular pylons. Only one of these is included, with the Leitch grandstand really being the focus of the image.

This book could be said to be self-indulgent, tongue in cheek, hopelessly uncommercial, ridiculously optimistic or a key visual record of amazingly varied structures. The reader will form their opinion.

Of course, Joni Mitchell was right to go on to sing:

Don't it always seem to go
That you don't know what you've got 'til it's gone.

Mike Floate
Crockenhill, March 2016

Contents:

The Underview 07
A visual record of floodlight pylons detailing their design and structure.

The Groundview 49
Floodlights featured within an image of the ground.

Getting to the Vetch Field 75
Views of the floodlights guiding fans to the Vetch Field, Swansea City.

At a Distance Foldout
After a game the floodlights at the Vetch Field seen from across the bay and the top of Townhill.

Brentford

2005

Darlington

2003

Cambridge United

2004

1997
Rotherham United

The
Underview

Barrow

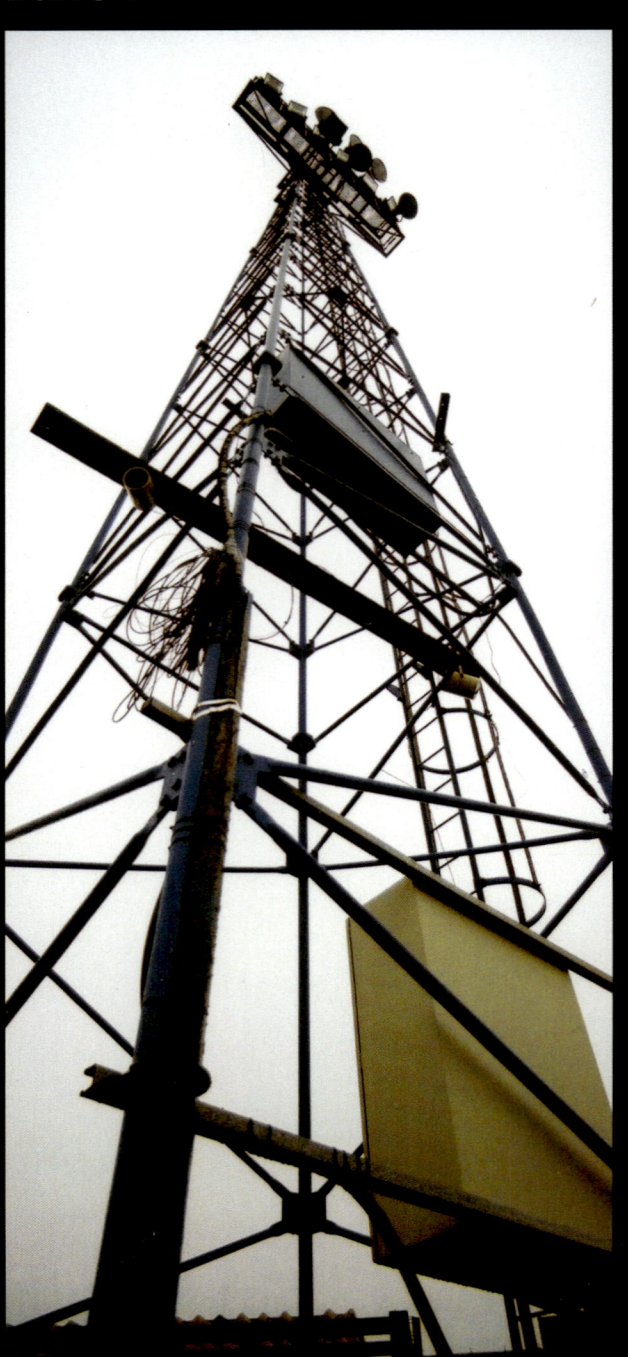

2004

08

Barnsley

Bristol Rovers

Brighton & Hove Albion

Blackpool

1998

Bolton Wanderers

Cardiff City

Chelmsford City

Carlisle United

Carlisle United

2008

17

Chesterfield

Enfield

Exeter City

Fulham

Hereford United

Hartlepool United

2008

23

Hull City

Hendon

2008

25

Nottingham Forest

Leyton Orient

Oxford United

Crystal Palace Stadium

Portsmouth

Plymouth Argyle

Shrewsbury Town

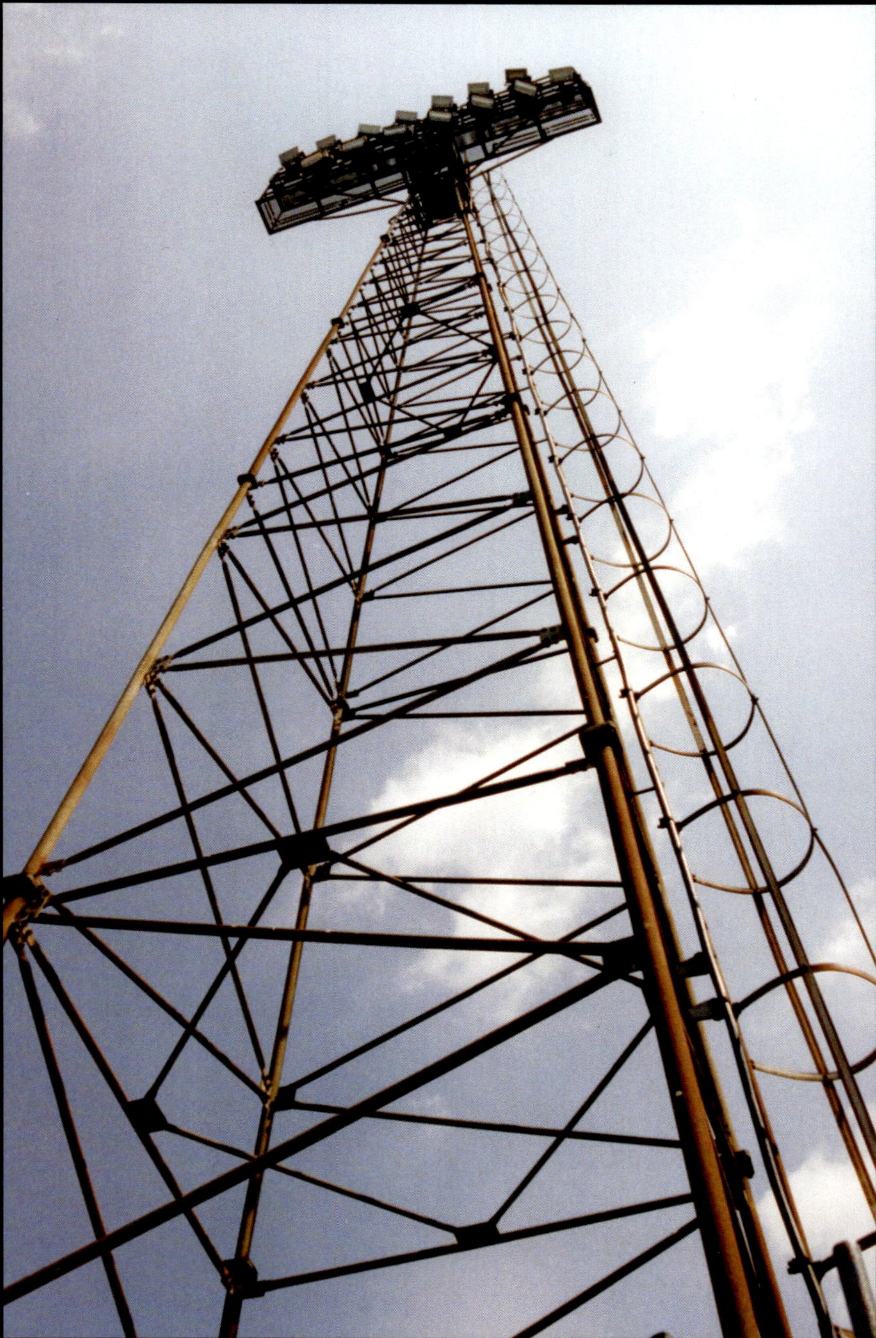

Swindon Town

1999

34

Swansea City

Wigan Athletic

Torquay United

Wimbledon

Wimbledon

2001

39

Workington

2004

Wrexham

Ayr United

Queen of the South

Royal Antwerp

St Mirren

KAA Gent

KSV Waregem

2006
Barnsley ———— 48

The
Groundview

Dundee

Chesterfield

Peterborough United

1999

52

Peterborough United

Bolton Wanderers

1998

54

Crystal Palace

2004

55

Queen of the South

… **Wimbledon**

Wimbledon

2001

58

KFC Winterslag

Portsmouth

Fulham

Dundee

KAA Gent

Portsmouth

Oxford United

Fulham

Oxford United

Hull City

Hull City

2002

69

Shrewsbury Town

2007

B&HAFC

1997

2003
Swansea City ———

Getting to the Vetch Field

2005

2005

74

2005

2003

2005

2005

2005

79

Index:

Ayr United	01
Barnsley	09, 49
Barrow	08
Blackpool	12
Bolton Wanderers	13, 54
Boston	04
Brentford	05
Brighton & HA	11, 71
Bristol Rovers	10
Cambridge United	05
Cardiff City	14
Carlisle	16, 17
Chelmsford	15
Chesterfield	18, 51
Crystal Palace	55
Crystal Palace Stadium	29
Darlington	5
Dundee	50, 62
Enfield	19
Exeter City	20
Fulham	21, 61, 66
Gent	46, 63
Hartlepool	23
Hastings United	1
Hendon	25
Hereford	22
Hull City	Back Cover, 24, 68, 69
Leyton Orient	27
Nottingham Forest	26
Oxford United	28, 65, 67
Peterborough	52, 53
Plymouth Argyle	31
Portsmouth	30, 60, 64
Queen of the South	43, 56
Reading	33
Rotherham United	6, 7
Shrewsbury	32, 70
Southampton	80
St Mirren	45
Swansea City	35, 72 - 79 & foldout
Swindon Town	34
Torquay United	Front Cover, 37
Waregem	47
Wigan Athletic	36
Wimbledon	38, 39, 57, 58
Winterslag	59
Workington	40
Wrexham	41

The Dell

2006

80